ELIJAH ON MY MIND

A LITTLE BOY WHO LOVES ME MORE THAN ANY MAN EVER COULD

Nina Marie Duran

Wyatt-MacKenzie Publishing, Inc.
DEADWOOD, OREGON

Elijah on My Mind: A Little Boy Who Loves Me More
Than Any Man Ever Could

by Nina Marie Duran

Photography by Daniel W. Torres Photography

Published by The Mom-Writers Publishing Cooperative
Wyatt-MacKenzie Publishing, Inc., Deadwood, OR
www.WyMacPublishing.com (541) 964-3314

Requests for permission or further information should be addressed to: Wyatt-MacKenzie Publishing, 15115 Highway 36, Deadwood, Oregon 97430

Printed in the United States of America

DEDICATION

To my mama, dad, Elijah,

and the brilliant Daniel San Miguel Jr.

INTRODUCTION

There were two important questions my dad would ask me when I was a little girl. One, "How do you spell excellent," and two, "What do you want to be when you grow up?" As a child, I never thought twice about either question. I would spell out e-x-c-e-l-l-e-n-t and then quickly say that I wanted to be a vegetarian. My father would laugh at these silly words that were uttered from my childish lips. Daddy knew that being a vegetarian wouldn't pay the bills, but I didn't. All I knew was that I wanted to be like my mom. She was a vegetarian so I wanted to be one too; little did I know at that time that mama was ordered by her oncologist to become a vegetarian. She was battling cancer and multiple sclerosis, and this was going to help her live a longer and healthier life.

Growing up, I spent a lot of time with my daddy. He would take me out all time so mama could rest. On the occasional days that I would stay with mama, she would make me write stories. She was very sneaky when it came to keeping me busy. She would tell me, "Nina, I want you to write me a story."

Since I loved balloons, I would grab my wide-ruled paper and begin to write away about them. One page, two page, and then hours later I would have my tenth page. Writing came easy to me, even at a young age. Mama would always tell me that God blessed me with a talent, but I never knew that it would have led me to the place where I am now.

Four years ago, I was in search for a true story. Not just any story, but one that I could relate to. I just found out I was pregnant and I was taken back to my childhood. You see, when I was little I would write stories that I couldn't read about. My parents would take me to the bookstore, but I never found children's books about balloons or about cancer. I had to write my own. This day I wanted a book or journal that was simple and yet unforgettable. I wanted to read about real women who had been in my shoes. I walked up and down the aisles and found nothing. I found books written by psychologists, doctors, and other professionals, but none that were written from a mother's heart. I was desperate. I left the bookstore feeling incomplete and unsatisfied. I drove home anxious to grab my pencil and paper. Soon, writing became my escape. I wrote all my thoughts during my pregnancy and even those after. This became a way for me to release my emotions.

This book is not a tale of postpartum depression, nor is it one written by a pediatrician, psychologist, or any other doctor for that matter. This is a collection of my thoughts. This is a journal which tells of a heart that wasn't ready to become a mother. A heart that wasn't ready to nurture another person...a heart that lacked responsibility...a heart that has been molded from all the ups and downs of motherhood.

I have gone through some very dark moments with my baby boy and I have experienced happiness at a level that only a mother can understand.

My life was interrupted, I became selfish, and then I learned how to love unconditionally...all because of a little boy named Elijah.

TABLE OF CONTENTS

CHAPTER ONE

LIFE INTERRUPTED

It was 2003 and the San Antonio Spurs were on their way to a 2nd World Championship. I was anxious to see if I had gotten the internship, but at the same time, scared. Elijah was four months old and I was taking 18 hours of undergraduate classes at the University of Incarnate Word. I wasn't sure if I could handle another responsibility but, before I could make any more decisions, I received a call from the San Antonio Spurs, offering me the internship that any student would kill for. It didn't get any better. I could go to every game and participate in any event that employees were invited to. There was only one catch…I had to be at each game, 6 hours prior, meaning if we had a game at 7 pm I had to be there by one in the afternoon.

I spoke to my parents about this opportunity and they vowed to help me with Elijah. Within days they hired a nanny and I was off to begin a long and sleepless journey.

I remember nights sitting at the computer with Elijah in my lap. I would rock him to sleep while doing homework or I would place him in his rocker right next to me. When it came time to feed him I would become so frustrated. I wanted him to swallow his food so I could get back to work. Most nights I cried. I was tired from work, school, and my marketing internship with the San Antonio Spurs. I felt helpless and I began to rethink all my decisions.

When I had initially found out that I was pregnant, a small part of me contemplated having an abortion for many reasons. One, I had just broken off an engagement with a guy…not the baby's daddy…someone else. As if that wasn't bad enough, I wasn't quite sure as to how I was going to break the news to my parents. I was unsure of their reaction and I was unsure of my capabilities. What if I didn't have what it took to be a mother? After all, I was far from perfect. I waited almost six hours before telling my mother that I was pregnant. Her reaction was not pleasant. She was disappointed and as soon as my father found out, he was just as hurt. Their "perfect" daughter had done wrong.

I knew the following months were going to be difficult, and they were. During the first couple months my mom would call me at all hours of the night. She was mad at me and this was her way of letting me know. Sometimes she was yelling at me and other times she would just cry on the phone. There were times when she would call me to tell me about the horrible nightmares she was having. Each dream involved me either swimming in oil, or having hard times breathing. She was worried, as would any mother, and how could I blame her. Sometimes I would ignore her phone calls, other times I couldn't... she would call over and over, until I answered and set her at ease. My dad, on the other hand, didn't talk to me for a while. He didn't want to see me and I couldn't blame him. I made his worst nightmare come true. If I were a dad, I would have probably reacted the same way. The day he did decide to break the silence, he took me into a conference room. I sat on one side of the desk and he sat on the other side. He was holding a notepad and a pen. He began speaking to me as if I were an employee. At first I wanted to laugh, but then I realized that this was his way of leveling with me without over-reacting. Months passed before they finally came around. My mom began to buy clothes for the unborn child, and my dad began to talk to me like a father again. Those were the hardest months. My parents mean the world to me and when I betrayed them, that world was shattered. It would take a long time before they trusted me again. Not only was I dealing with my own emotions, but I was also dealing with my parents'. Despite everything, when I had Elijah times only got harder.

I remember getting out of the shower one evening. It was colder than usual and my naked feet hit the bathroom tile. I looked at myself in the mirror, but instead I saw Elijah in the background. He was sound asleep on the bed in his boppy. I grabbed my towel and began to wipe my drenched hair. I walked towards him and I began to cry. I felt a sense of helplessness that I had never in my life felt. I looked at him over and over again, examining his tiny body. His life depended on me. If I didn't feed him, he would die. If I didn't care for him, he would perish. If I didn't nurture him and love him, it would have life-long effects. I remember hurting inside. My chest was tight and my stomach was in knots. I was not ready for this. I was too young. I felt alone…more lonely that I had ever felt.

My life was interrupted and there was nothing I could do about it. He was the street and I was standing on the sidewalk. This was a choice that I made. No one twisted my arm. I knew what I was doing; I just had no idea how difficult it was going to be. My days and nights were blurred. Sleep was impossible. Taking a shower or putting on makeup became a luxury. If I had time to shower twice a week, I was more than happy. If I had a moment to make nachos I would enjoy each bite. My time, my life, and my heart were consumed by this little baby whom I loved before I even laid eyes on him.

My new life with Elijah was different. It was challenging and I knew that I had to do everything possible to make my parents and those around me keep their faith in me. From day one, I said that I was going to graduate from college. I promised my parents that nothing would stop me. Even though I know they had faith in me, I still believed there was a seed of doubt.

During my pregnancy I continued attending classes. I was taking 21 hours the semester before Elijah was born. It was tough. I remember one day being late to class. I was running up the stairs and I slipped. I walked into the classroom with tears in my eyes and much to my surprise the teacher was sympathetic. That day I was supposed to give a presentation, but was allowed another day. While I was pregnant, I was one of those women that would sleep all the time. My energy level was low and doing homework was always a challenge. There were times I would search the Internet to see if I could pay someone to do my work…but I never had the guts to go through with it.

Spring semester, 2003, will always be what I call, the "spring of my life." Elijah was born on the 23rd of January and my last semester began on the 20th. I was so worried that I was not going to keep my promise. I made sure to contact each and every one of my professors. I told them my situation and they all agreed to help me. I graduated with my bachelor's degree in August of 2003. That spring and summer will always remain unforgettable; the San Antonio Spurs won the

NBA World Championship, I had graduated, and Elijah was now 8 months old. In my mind I was ready to find a job and begin to work full-time, but God had another plan for me. Mid-September I received a letter from the University of Incarnate Word regarding graduate school. I read it and then put it aside…and then read it again. After thinking about it, I asked my father his opinion, even though I knew what he was going to say.

That October I started graduate school. I began taking classes in the evening. The first couple of semesters I was in school Monday and Wednesday from 6pm till 10pm. Life was hard. I had papers due every class period, exams to study for, and presentations to place together. I was obligated to meet with people for group projects and I needed to be sure to find time for everything. Within a 24-hour period I was a mother, employee, friend, and student. I felt like a schizophrenic. I was living so many different lives at once. Sometimes when I think about it, I have no idea how I did everything. I never took any energy supplements and I never took any medications to battle depression (after all, I wasn't depressed…just confused). Somehow, through prayer and the prayer of others around me, I was able to find a way.

Even though I was living a good life, I always felt like I had no time for myself. When I was with Elijah I remember getting antsy and frustrated when he would cry. When he was first born he came down with colic for almost two weeks. Any parent that has ever had a child with colic knows how difficult it is to deal with. Elijah would cry, and cry, and cry. There were nights when I would stand in the restroom, holding the blow dryer because the noise would stop him from crying…or maybe it would just drown out his tears. Sometimes I would turn on the shower and sit next to the toilet just so I could hear the water running instead of his tears running. Discovering white noise was helpful. For some reason it would stop him from crying and put him to sleep. I remember lying there in bed with him at my side wishing that I had made another decision…praying that I could reverse time. The hardest part about being a mother at that moment was wondering if I was the only one who felt like that. Did other moms experience this sadness and regret? Or was I simply being selfish? Either way, I went through it.

The feeling of resentment was real for me. I loved my son, but I also wanted my old life back.

One day I was browsing through quotes on the internet when I came across one that read as follows: What if finding the love of your life meant changing the life that you love? I kept reading it over and over.

This quote was somehow made for me. My life had been interrupted without warning. God gave me Elijah…but when He did, He took away my old life and blessed me with a new one. Now all I needed to do was find out why and find a way to get over my selfishness and become the best mother that I could possibly be.

CHAPTER TWO

SELFISH ME

It is so easy for the selfish side of me to creep up and want a single life without a child. Before Elijah I didn't really go out much, but I was able to live my life at my own pace and not worry about anyone else. Everything changed when Elijah was born. My time was now his time. My life was now his life. My schedule revolved around his schedule. I was hit by a freight train when he was born. Why is it that when I had the time to go out and be wild I never did? And now that my friends were calling me to go grab a drink, I couldn't? At times, God works in the most mysterious ways. I remember feeling this sense of craziness that wanted to burst inside me. I was there feeding my child, wishing I could be out at the bars taking shots with my friends. What kind of mother thinks this way? Apparently, many do.

When Elijah was first born I was too busy to go

out. I was still in school, I was working, and I was also interning with the San Antonio Spurs. But the time I had to myself was only given to me because of my parents. They were nice enough to hire help. A lady by the name of Rosa graced our lives. Every morning when Elijah would wake up at 6 in the morning, I could take him downstairs and go right back up for a few more hours of sleep. He would watch Baby Einstein and I would be upstairs, sleeping. It was great. I had so many hands helping me, but eventually I was spoiled. I wanted more time. I wanted time to go see a movie and time to go dance. Sometimes I would lie just to get out of the house. Before I knew it, I began to neglect my son. I loved my time with my friends and I wanted that every weekend. I wanted to drop Elijah off and head out like every other normal 24 year-old, 23 at the time. At first I didn't feel bad. I felt good. I was going out, living the single life, and then being a mother when I chose to. I would spend the night all over the place. I never knew where I would end up at the end of the night so I always had a bag with extra clothes. There were nights when we would go out and I would charge 70 dollars worth of liquor on my debit card, even when I knew I had diapers and other necessities to purchase. Elijah was not on the top of my priority list. He was second to my personal life. There were even nights when I would pick him up from one babysitter and take him to another. In one day he would have as many as three different people taking care of him. Inside I knew that what I was doing was wrong…but it was hard to stop. In fact, it lasted almost one year.

It's funny how reality hits at the most inopportune times. I remember lying on a friend's couch one Sunday morning after partying the night before. That night we had a thunderstorm that passed through, probably waking up every neighborhood in San Antonio. My cell phone rang, and it was my mom. Most days I would let it go to voicemail, but this time I decided to answer it. I could tell she was crying and immediately I thought something was wrong. My mom asked me one question…

"Nina, do you remember what you used to do when it thundered?"

I stayed silent and let her talk.

"Whenever we had a big storm, you would run to our room and jump in bed with your father and me," she said. "And it breaks my heart that Elijah didn't have you to run to last night."

She hung up the phone and my eyes began to water. How many tears am I going to shed before I realize that what I am doing is wrong? She was right. Elijah was probably terrified and I was nowhere near him. If he tried running to me, he wasn't going to find me. If he wanted to cuddle with me for comfort, I wasn't going to be there. If he needed his momma to tell him that the storm won't hurt him, it wasn't going to happen. Instead he was going to find the arms of a babysitter…the arms of someone who would never love him like I did…the arms of someone temporary.

I sat there on the couch contemplating my life and my decisions (again). I was so mad at myself and I couldn't pinpoint a reason. Was I mad because I had a child? Was I mad because I was neglecting my son? Was I just being flat out selfish? What was it? Why did I feel this way? Although I wanted to leave at that second, I didn't want my friends knowing my situation. So I hung out, ate some tacos, and then left to go pick up Elijah from his babysitter. I pulled up slowly and honked my horn. It took seconds for him to run outside and greet me. He smiled. He was so happy to see me, and I was happy to see him. I sat him in his car seat and we went home.

I spent that entire day with him. We went to the store, to the park, and then to Blockbuster to rent some movies. Throughout the day I would look at him and think to myself, "wow, I am so selfish…why would any-one want to leave this little boy." From that moment on I have tried my best to spend as much time with him as possible. I never wanted to feel that sense of helpless-ness again. I wanted him to know that momma loved him more than life itself and if anyone wanted my time, they needed to take a number.

CHAPTER THREE

SLEEPING BABY, RESTLESS MOMMA

When I was six months pregnant I went to the doctor for my first ultrasound. I was so excited to find out the gender of my baby. I wanted a boy more than anything in the world. As the radiologist was taking pictures, I noticed instantly it was a boy. My heart filled with happiness. My body was consumed by a feeling which to date, I cannot explain. After every photo was taken I walked upstairs to see my OBGYN. She came in the room and began to explain all the small, yet significant details. Everything was looking great...well, almost everything. She began to tell me the baby's brain wasn't developing properly. She pointed out a tiny hole that measured less than 2 centimeters, however, she told me I had a few options.

Option # 1: I could have an abortion.

Option # 2: I could take classes that would teach

me how to raise a child that was mentally challenged.

Option # 3: I could go see a specialist and leave everything else in God's hands.

I chose Option # 3, which in my opinion was the hardest of the three. I went to see a specialist and was told that there was a small chance of having a baby with Down Syndrome, but there was also a chance of him having no problems at all. I decided to continue my journey with my ever-growing belly. It was tough emotionally and spiritually. I would stay up at night praying that God would take care of this soul that resided in my belly. I would break down and cry at work or in school. I was consumed and yet I kept telling myself that faith is greater than science. Sure enough, by God's grace, Elijah was born and he was healthy. He was perfect…and he was mine.

Still, even after be was born…I continued to be restless.

When Elijah was first born, I was terrified of SIDS (Sudden Infant Death Syndrome). Each night I had to sleep with him next to me. My mind wasn't at ease if he was in another room or another bed. What if he stopped breathing? What if he cries and I can't hear him? So many horrible thoughts would flood my brain. Even when he was sleeping I was restless. I never wanted to get comfortable for the fear that I would fall asleep and miss any little move that he made. During the day it was a little easier to sleep. He would take small naps and I would join him. Together we would dream…and snore. I'm not sure what he was dreaming of, but I can tell you that my cat naps were so peaceful I could care less if I was dreaming or not. Most of the time Elijah and I would sleep on the couch. I felt safe in that small space with him pressed up against my chest. When I could, I would sleep with my shirt off and I would take off his as well. I would press his body against mine so we could feel each other breathing. The few times that I was awake while he slept I would watch the TLC Channel. I was consumed with A Baby Story, A Wedding Story, and all the other shows that would come on. I never changed the channel…it stayed on TLC for hours and hours at a time, even while we slept.

Days and nights were pretty much nonexistent when Elijah was born. All I had was sunshine and darkness. Hours and minutes no longer mattered. I didn't have an agenda; I just had things to do. When Elijah slept, I worried. When he was awake, I worried. It seems as if worry was the only constant. There were so many nights when I would stay awake thinking of everything I had to do as a mother. I needed money. I needed formula. I needed time. Everything seemed so far from my reach. I wanted to stay positive, but it was hard. Here I was trying to lose what I call "baby fat" and at the same time deal with my present situation. I was in debt. I owed the hospital over four thousand dollars. Apparently insurance doesn't cover emergency deliveries. I owed on my all my credit cards. I had a Visa, Discover, and Master Card that were all overdrawn and well past due and calculating everything only made matters worse. I was over fifteen thousand dollars in debt and I had no idea how to get ahead. I spent so much of my energy wondering how I was going to pay bills. I was at a place where I had no money and nowhere to go. Sure I could go to my parents, but I had done that time and time again throughout college. My face would wrinkle from crying so many tears. Until that time, I thought only my hands and feet could wrinkle. I had never cried so much in my entire life. Even though my heart was complete, it felt broken. Here I was, a new mother, blessed with a healthy little baby, and yet I was so sad. Why? He was healthy! That's all that ever mattered to me. Somehow all the financial stress managed to blind me of everything positive in my life. When I was up at night, stressing, Elijah was sleeping. As soon as I would hit the sack, he would wake up...that was just my luck. But, I learned how to deal with it. I learned how to handle the late nights and the restless evenings.

Nowadays Elijah sleeps very well. Normally he goes to bed around 9pm and then he's out for the entire night but, it's been three years and I am still dealing with the same restlessness. I still stay up at night staring at his innocence. There are nights when I wake up at 1:00 in the morning and go to the computer to check my bank account. The majority of the time it's overdrawn. I have paid so many overdraft fees that I have literally lost count. It's really sad when I deposit $1,000 in my bank account and when I get my current balance it is only $300 because it was negative $700. Once I've noticed my debt, I begin to click on every lender I can find. I apply for loans and credit cards even though I know that I am not going to get approved. If I do get approved I have to put down a deposit or I only get a $200 limit, which doesn't help...in fact it worsens matters. I sit there, helpless, and think of everything I can possibly do. Most of the time, I just have to accept it and sign off. After I've been sitting at the computer for a few hours I begin to cry (again). And then I talk out loud to myself. I say things like, "get it together, Nina"...and "this too shall pass"...before I know it my tears begin to fade. I sneak back into my room and fall asleep, knowing that even though I'm going to wake up in debt, I am also going to wake up with the most beautiful little boy by my side.

CHAPTER FOUR

STRETCH MARKS, STRETCH MARKS GO AWAY

Each morning I would wake up and look at my expanding belly in the mirror. I would examine my belly button and all the crazy shapes that my tummy was taking on. One day it looked like a square and the next day it was shaped like a pear. I found it cute. I thought my tummy was somewhat sexy and defined me as a woman. There was someone growing inside me that needed to stretch and make my stomach home.

I remember standing sideways in the mirror and noticing a small red mark on the bottom of my belly. I could barely see it, but I knew it was a stretch mark. When I was in middle school, I remember getting stretch marks because I was exercising and my legs were getting "thick"…I hated it…and now they were back (well, one at least). As the days passed I kept noticing more and more of these little blemishes on my belly.

They were growing vertically and several were appearing at a time.

The next time I went to visit my OBGYN I asked her if there was any way to prevent more from appearing. She nicely told me that more than likely, I would continue to see them and the chances of them fading were slim to none. Great...just great...how am I supposed to be a sexy momma if I have these marks tattooing my stomach? Although I should have accepted them at that time, I was certain that through prayer and faith, they would go away.

Before you begin to freak out and wonder if stretch marks are going to plague you, let me let you in on a little secret. I gained almost 70 pounds when I was pregnant. Ok, so it's not really a secret. If you've been doing your research, you will already know that that is not healthy. Even though I didn't start gaining weight till my 7th month, I caught up very quickly. The average pregnant woman should only gain between 15 and 30 pounds. I well exceeded that limit, but I couldn't help it. If I had three blueberry donuts sitting on my desk, I would eat all three. If I saw 12 cookies in the break

room, I would eat the dozen and save none for later.
Some of my favorite meals were as follows: Ramen
Noodle, Frutti Pebbles cereal, and Girl Scout Thin
Mints. Sometimes I would eat all of that in one serving.
I always seemed to have room for more food. I used
the "eating for two" excuse more than anyone I know.
I love food as it is, and being pregnant gave me an
opportunity to eat as much as I wanted. I ate and ate
and ate…and I have all the stretch marks to prove it!

Three years have gone by and I am still getting
use to having blemishes on my belly. You would think
that by now I would be comfortable with my body, but
I'm not. I have tried every cream and every treatment
(within my budget) to try and rid of my marks. One
time I even paid 15 dollars on a website to get a home
remedy. That night I remember mixing salt, sugar, mud,
and other substances together in a bowl. The idea was to
mix it all together and then rub it all over my stomach
vigorously in the shower for 15 minutes. I did this over
and over for days. The only thing that came from that
remedy was irritated stretch marks and a sore stomach.
I have purchased creams that cost hundreds of dollars

and all I have now are empty tubes and crusted tops.

Every morning I get dressed in the mirror. I could tell you that I have accepted my stretch marks, but then I would be lying to you. Others accept them, but I can't. It's really hard to feel sexy when I know that I have this problem. I see other women that wear shirts that bare a little skin and I'm jealous. I see women wearing bikinis and I cringe when I try on bathing suits. I see women looking beautiful in lingerie and all I want is to look the same way. Magazines and television taunt me. I see women that are flawless and even though I am aware of the power of digital photography, I still want to look like them. Now, don't get me wrong, I have learned to live with my stretch marks. I have learned to cover them up and still look somewhat sexy. In all honesty, most people that see me probably have no idea that I have stretch marks…but I do. I see them in the morning and I see them in the afternoon. I see them in the evening and underneath the moon. When I go to the restroom, I see them. When I set foot in a dressing room, I see them. When I take off my clothes, I see them. When I shower, I see them. Sometimes I even catch myself talking to my stomach!

"Can't you just go away?"

But they don't. No matter how much I pray or how many remedies I try, they have become an extension of my body.

Even Elijah will ask me, "Momma, what's that on your tummy?"

I calmly, yet sarcastically tell him, while pointing at my tummy, "Oh, honey…that…those are marks that momma got when she was pregnant with you."

And then he makes me feel better by telling me, "I'm sorry momma, you want a band-aid?"

CHAPTER FIVE

"MOMMA, I WAITED FOR YOU"

It was a Tuesday morning and the sun was still hiding. Elijah and I had been up almost all night battling a cough that took over his fragile body. Instead of getting better, his cough was only worsening.

It had been almost a month now and he had gone through three antibiotics and other over-the-counter medication. I was frustrated and worn. As soon as the sunlight arose from its sleep, I decided to get dressed and take Elijah to the emergency room. I needed to know what was wrong with him. I left him in his pajamas and we were off to the local children's hospital.

We arrived at the hospital within ten minutes. The nurse took all his vitals and placed us in a private room. I sat there patiently while Elijah examined his surroundings. He didn't even look sick. He was jumping on the chairs and touching everything within his reach. When the doctor entered the room she began to ask a million questions. Has he had fever? Has he had any vomiting? Is he lethargic?

Yes...Yes...and No.

Lethargic?!?! In three years, I don't think Elijah has ever been lethargic. He's had fever...he's been sick to his stomach...but none of that could stop his energetic soul. If you think the Energizer bunny can keep going and going, wait till you meet Elijah. As she began to diagnose him and listen to his chest, she noticed that he was wheezing. She gave him four treatments, and before I knew it, he was coughing less and sounded much better. His diagnoses...asthma. I left the hospital feeling a little bit better and so did Elijah. Before we even left the hospital parking lot, he was sound asleep in his car seat.

As I was driving home, I was anxious to place him in bed and sleep with him. The both of us had a bad night and we were due for a long nap. I got home and took him down from the car. When I walked into our room he got up and told me he was no longer tired. As much as I tried to convince him, he was ready to play with his toys and watch movies, so we did. We played all day. We went outside, we played with the dogs, we did the laundry, we got on the computer, we danced, and did everything else his little heart desired.

Before I knew it, hours had passed. By this time it was almost 4pm. I was drained and I know Elijah was just as tired. He was fussy and he was really testing my patience. Anyone who is a parent knows that eventually our patience runs out. There comes a point in every mother's life when you want to close the door on your children and never listen to their tears or whines again. That was me. I was ready to explode. I was frustrated, tired, and worn. I went to my momma's room and asked her for help. I told her that I needed to leave the house and get some fresh air, even if it was only for 30 minutes. She told me to put Elijah to bed and as soon as he fell asleep I was free to go.

About 7pm, Elijah finally decided to get under the blankets and fall asleep. By this time he was crying and so was I. We we're both exhausted. Before he fell asleep he asked me if I was going to be there when he woke up, and of course I said, "Yes." I left the house and began to drive to the movies to meet a friend. Tears flooded my face as I drove to the theatre. I was so upset and mad at Elijah.

Why couldn't he just sleep?

Why did he have to be so demanding?

Why can't he just leave me alone?

All these questions were taunting my mind and filling me with guilt. I finally arrived at the theatre and walked in as the movie was beginning. I must have stayed only 45 minutes before walking out. I was sitting there watching a comedy and yet my heart felt tragically sad. I left Elijah at home and I felt bad. I politely told my friend that I was leaving and I snuck out. As I was walking out of the movie I called my mom to let her know that I was coming home. She began to laugh and told me, "Nina, you and this little boy have a very special connection." Apparently, Elijah had just woken up and was heartbroken because I had left him. I told my mom to take him to the window and tell him that I was on my way home.

I pulled into the driveway and saw Elijah's little face poking out of the blinds. He was sad, tired, and happy all at once. His tears told me he was sad. His red

"So this is Love"

Elijah is now three years old and the classic Cinderella is his #1 movie. We watch it before he goes to school, when he comes home from school, and before he goes to sleep. Every now and then he'll switch it up and say, "Nemo," but that's very rare. Children are very unique in that way. Once they like something, they are dedicated for a period of time. Currently, Elijah is dedicated to Cinderella. It's cute. I don't know how he has the patience to see the same movie again and again. On top of that, each time he watches it, he asks the same questions, and he watches it with such enthusiasm. It always seems like it's his first time. Since I am his mother, I always watch it with him. We lie there together and laugh at all the parts we laughed at the day before and the day before that day and the day before that day.

I always seem to have great thoughts at weird times. It wasn't too long ago when we were watching

Cinderella and something hit me. It was during the scene where the prince and Cinderella are dancing. There is a song that is playing entitled "So this is Love." I began to listen to the words and I was amazed. They were so simple, yet so true. I can't type them for copyright reasons, but I can quote the one line that touched me.

"So this is love, so this is what makes life divine."

Another word for divine is "heavenly." I can honestly say that Elijah has made my life heavenly. When everyone else is mad at me, Elijah is not. When everyone else has given up on me, Elijah is still there. When everyone else has better plans, Elijah's only plan is to be with me. My self-esteem has been like a roller coaster. It has been up and down many times. When Elijah was first born I was lower than dirt. Now, when I look at my life and what I have done, I am higher than cloud nine. Although many trying times have come from having a child, many beautiful times have come as well. I have battled with my decisions and I have struggled with regret. Only time and God can heal a broken heart and a broken spirit. Three years have passed and many things have changed. I have learned how to love this little boy unconditionally. He holds every key to my heart. Looking back, I can now say that I was selfish. Do I blame myself? No. To me, it was a part of growing up. I learned from my mistakes. I have taken them all to heart. At the same time, I have learned to leave many things at the altar. Because of prayer and faith from my family, I have made it through some tough hurdles. I learned how to break down walls, and I learned how to make the best of the worst situation.

Before reading the final chapter of my book, I would like to shed words of wisdom upon you…

If I had any advice to give to momma's reading this book it would be as follows:

❀ Always look for the sweet in life, but realize that you can't take away the bitter.

❀ Cling to prayer and faith…sometimes they are all you've got.

❀ Don't ever feel sorry for yourself…that will only make it harder.

❀ Focus on the beautiful moments and that which is present, not past.

❀ Remember, the darkest moments are when the stars shine brightest.

❀ Surround yourself with positive people and positive energy as much as possible.

❀ Express your feelings, even if that means screaming and crying.

❀ Be inspired by your abilities as a mother, not everyone is as blessed as you are.

❀ Love your child unconditionally.

❀ Know that many women are in your shoes and you are not alone.

❀ Learn how to laugh at your mistakes instead of losing sleep over them.

❀ Challenge yourself to be a better mother.

❀ Forget about all the diets. Eat healthy and in portions, and the fat will melt away.

❀ Sadness is contagious; don't pass it on to other mothers.

❀ Last but not least, love is the only language a child can understand. Be sure to speak clearly each and every day to your children, even when you would rather close the door.

CHAPTER SEVEN

ELIJAH ON MY MIND

Since Elijah has been in my life, dull moments do not exist. He can add spice to anything, anyone, and any place. He has a smile that can melt a cold heart, and a presence that makes the old feel young. No one...and I mean no one, can make my heart break and mend as quickly as he can. To me, he has magical powers that he has yet to reveal. He's manipulative in an honest way, and he's sneaky in a cute and sincere manner. He can make me believe that I bought him a present, even though I didn't. He can make me eat tacos, even when I don't feel like tacos. He can make me watch Dora the Explorer, even when I don't want to watch cartoons. What is it about this little boy? He has such a hold on me...but I love it.

When Elijah was first born, he was the only baby with hair...lots of hair. All the other newborns were bald. Elijah stood out. He was quiet and had this secret to him. When he first blessed this world with his physical body, he wasn't crying. The doctor placed him on my chest and told me to hold him, so I did. It wasn't until they began poking his little feet that he began to shed tears and shout for help. He must have been so scared. He was in an unknown world and it was up to me to make this place his home. As soon as they swaddled him, he was placed in my arms. I remember his big head and his stillness. He was safe, and he felt it. He was loved, and he knew it. They took him from me and ran more tests. During that period of time I went up to my private room and waited patiently for him. Thoughts ran through my head. He was here. Elijah was here.

When they brought Elijah to me I began to breastfeed him. That was frustrating and yet spiritual. This was my way of connecting on an intimate level with Elijah. We were bonding. I remember watching him latch on. It was so beautiful. He was so tiny and yet he knew what to do. Although I wanted to, it didn't last long. Within two weeks I began to feed him formula and I stopped breastfeeding. I wasn't consuming enough food and my schedule was not permitting the time needed to pump. At first I was sad, but then I realized that food was food.

Elijah began to develop personality only weeks after he was born. He had this crooked smile that would appear on his face whenever I sang to him. When he was hungry he would look for things to suck on and when he was tired he would dig his head in dark places. He was so cute to watch. As his eyesight developed he would focus on lights, and other bright objects. Anything moving brought him pleasure. The first DVD I ever bought him was a Baby Einstein DVD. This video had snazzy noises, vibrant puppets, and soothing music. He would watch this video every morning when he would wake up. There were many times I saw it with him, just to see what he was laughing at.

When I think of "first times" I can recall so many with Elijah.

❀ I remember the first time he smiled and stole my heart without asking permission.

❀ I remember the first time he got sick and shook my entire world.

❀ I remember the first time I washed his little body

with the gentlest soap on the market.

❀ I remember the first time I fell asleep with him on my naked chest, creating a bond that would never be broken.

❀ I remember the first time he stood up in his crib and I was so happy for him.

❀ I remember the first time he took a few steps and thought he was a king.

❀ I remember the first time he fell off the bed, making me feel like a bad momma.

❀ I remember the first time he reached up for me, wanting no one else.

❀ I remember the first time he called me "momma"…it was priceless.

❀ I remember the first time he threw a basketball; I knew he was going to make the pros.

❀ I remember the first time he began to dance with rhythm that was right on tune.

❀ I remember his first birthday; he could care less about the presents (he just wanted the wrapping paper).

❀ I remember his first head injury; I was scared out of

my mind and didn't know what to do.

❀ I remember the first time he slept through the night, which was peace on earth at its best.

❀ I could go on and on about everything I remember, but that would take a lifetime of writing. Elijah has blessed me with the fondest memories and he's only three years old. I can only imagine what else is in store.

This is Elijah on my mind

ACKNOWLEDGEMENTS

I would like to thank the following companies and
individuals who have helped support me
and this book.

Ramon Chapa

Elva's Pallet

Alice and Roland Fuentes

Chris and Rose Moran

Rich Rivera, *Sr. Corporate Executive of Verizon Business*

Richard A. Villanueva

Valerie Lucio Polk
May Kay - Independent Senior Sales Director
marykay.com/vallucio

AFTERWORD

Elijah was born on January 23, 2003. Carlos and I had only known each other for a year and within that time we got pregnant, got married, moved in together, and had a baby. It was too much for any couple. The first year of Elijah's life is still a blur to me. During that time I was regretting all my decisions, but I kept them within. I couldn't tell Carlos and I was fearful that my friends and family would think badly of me. Instead, I would cry when I was alone and hope that one day I would wake up from this dream. I didn't understand why I placed my life and decisions in the hands of others. All I wanted to do was go back in time and slow things down, but it was too late. If I told Carlos anything, I was scared that he would place all the blame on himself, when in actuality it was me. He was doing everything right. He was working late nights, going to school, and being a dad anytime he had a minute. I was the one doubting my decisions…I was the one who wanted to go home and be alone…I was the one that wanted to erase my past and create a new beginning.

My marriage didn't last long. Carlos and I fought often and instead of resolving anything, we'd place it behind us and move on. Or at least, I would. So much of my time was consumed by Elijah. Before I could blink my eyes, Carlos and I were living in separate houses. I moved back in with my mom and dad and he stayed at the house. We would talk almost every day, but we would also argue. I was upset and he was hurt. No matter how hard he tried, my ears were closed. I made up my mind and I didn't want to go back.

Things between Carlos and I were bad. We'd argue…we'd cry…we'd curse at each other…and at times, we wouldn't speak to each other for weeks. He had his reasons and I had mine. Although recently things between he and I have smoothed out, there are still times when we're at each other's neck. All in all, we both realize that we have a beautiful baby boy together, and nothing can change that. Even though every day is a battle, we are working to have a good relationship with one another. Some days are tougher than others, but in the long run, we both know that Elijah will always be the tie that keeps us bonded. Nowadays we share Elijah, equally. We both see him three to four times a week and we're both involved in his life.

When a relationship begins with lies, it's destined to end in disaster…but even disasters must be cleaned. Sometimes this can take weeks….months…. or even years. While cleaning up, there is no telling what you may find, so be prepared. Be ready to get your hands dirty and to spend a lot of time on your knees…praying. For both Carlos and me, prayer and keeping a relationship with God has been key to moving on with different lives with one thing in common…Elijah.

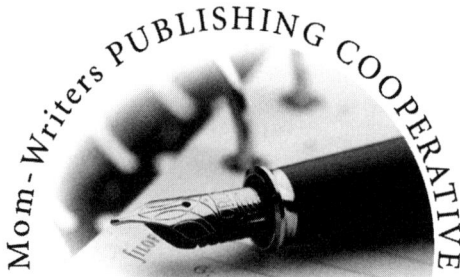

Mom-Writers PUBLISHING COOPERATIVE

We empower mom writers.

Publishing the Works of Extraordinary Mom Writers

Wyatt-MacKenzie Publishing, Inc

WyMacPublishing.com